It Snows on Wednesdays: Glass Island

Author:

Madelyn Rose Banta

It Snows on Wednesdays: Glass Island

Ilustrator: Theodore Rosen

Format: Rocio Monroy

Dedication

Madelyn Rose, we cannot be more proud of the young woman you have blossomed into. Though once just a small, innocent girl sitting in her kindergarten assessment, being asked, "Madelyn, when does it snow?" and without hesitation and with the upmost confidence, you replied, "Wednesday's!" with a bright, captivating smile!

That same boundless enthusiasm and unwavering spirit have only grown stronger with each passing year, shining through in the warmth of your gaze and the infectious joy of your bubbly personality. Your blue eyes sparkle with an almost otherworldly wonder, drawing in all who have the privilege of knowing you.

But it is your heart, your priceless, precious heart, that truly sets you apart - a gift from God, overflowing with kindness, empathy, and a profound understanding of the world that God has created.

To know Madelyn Rose is to know the best of humanity, a testament to the remarkable young woman she has become and the even brighter future that lies ahead.

Determined to save her community, Maddie snuck out through the melt before her parents' planned trip above the next morning.

16

Maddie was a young Glass Islander who spent her days marveling at the world above her icy home.

5

From below the frozen surface, she would paint the bellies of ducks and the blades of ice skates gliding by.

Though life bustled on Glass Island, with islanders going to school and work, Maddie dreamed of what it would be like above.

Each Wednesday brought wondrous snowfall that coated the ice in a blanket of white.

Maddie eagerly awaited these snowy days, which then gave way to Thursdays when the ice skaters would return, and she could once again see their skates swooping above.

As Maddie grew older,
she noticed changes in the
reliable Wednesday snows.

10

**The flakes looked different –
slushier and less fluffy.**

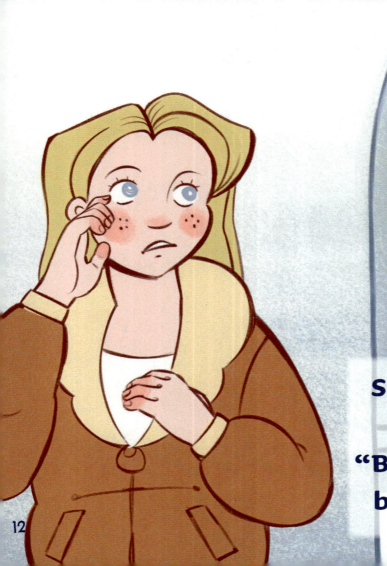

She overheard her parents' grave discussions of the "Big Melt" and the litter left behind by careless visitors.

Each year, the brilliant sun beat down hotter, melting more snow than could be replaced.

13

Without enough snow, the islanders couldn't build ice homes or sled down the frosted hills.

14

Maddie realized the survival of Glass Island depended on the actions of those above.

15

As they nervously emerged, they found Maddie surrounded by islanders, passionately explaining the Glass Islanders' concern.

17

She described their love of seeing duck feet gliding above and their sadness at the trash and melting ice.

18

She reminded them, "it snows on Wednesdays," and they all must care for the land they share.

Her parents watched proudly as Maddie brought the crowd together, securing their promise to keep the land clean so Glass Island could thrive.

They agreed to deliver snow each Wednesday and celebrate afterwards with cocoa and skating.

The islanders prepared joyfully for the next snowy Wednesday, working to restore their beautiful home.

Maddie's brave actions proved she would grow into a strong leader who could make a real difference!

23

Made in the USA
Middletown, DE
18 November 2024